Writing Skills Made Fun

Parts of Speech

BY KAREN KELLAHER

SCHOLASTIC
PROFESSIONAL BOOKS

NEW YORK • TORONTO • LONDON • AUCKLAND • SYDNEY

MEXICO CITY • NEW DELHI • HONG KONG • BUENOS AIRES

To Mary Kellaher, my dear mother-in-law,

and in loving memory of Donald Kellaher

Cover, interior, and poster art by Mike Moran
Front cover, interior, and poster design by Kathy Massaro

ISBN: 0-439-22268-0
Copyright © 2001 by Karen Kellaher.
Published by Scholastic Inc.

Contents

Writing Skills Made Fun: About the Series

As a writer and editor in the field of educational publishing, I frequently talk with language-arts teachers about the kinds of tools they need most. I also spend a lot of time browsing in bookstores and paging through teacher catalogs, checking out what is currently available. One thing I noticed over the past several years is that when it came to nitty-gritty writing skills, second- and third-grade teachers' needs were simply not being met. Sure, there were plenty of grammar and writing resources available to teachers of grades 5, 6 and above. But I saw very little quality material that was just right for the early elementary grades. I wrote this series to fill that "grammar gap"— and to assist you in your all-important mission of teaching the rules of writing.

As you are well aware, your job is cut out for you. According to state and national standards, by the time students enter second grade, they are expected to know and understand the basic rules of English grammar—and to consistently apply those rules to their own writing. Just take a look at some of the standards nationwide:

* **CALIFORNIA:** Second-graders must be able to distinguish between complete and incomplete sentences, use commas and quotation marks, and know when to capitalize letters. Third-graders in the Golden State must be able to use all four types of sentences, identify subjects and verbs, understand agreement and verb tenses, and identify and use all parts of speech.

* **ILLINOIS:** By the third grade, students should be able to construct complete sentences that demonstrate subject-verb agreement, use punctuation and capitalization properly, know and use the parts of speech, and demonstrate focus and organization when writing paragraphs.

* **TEXAS:** State standards dictate that by grade 3, "Students will recognize and demonstrate appropriate use of standard English: usage, mechanics, spelling, and sentence structure."

As you know, with tough standards come tough tests. Almost all major standardized tests for third-graders include sections on usage and mechanics. And many tests include open-ended writing sections that require students to demonstrate a working knowledge of the basic rules of grammar.

This book series, *Writing Skills Made Fun* is one way to help you meet these curriculum demands and make grammar fun. The series includes three books: *Parts of Speech*; *Capitalization, Punctuation & Spelling*; and *Sentences and Paragraphs*.

Parts of Speech

Many teachers remember the Schoolhouse Rock grammar skits that aired on Saturday morning TV during the 1970s and '80s. An entire generation of children grew up singing "A noun is a person, place or thing" and "Lolly, Lolly, Lolly, get your adverbs here!" Why did the learning come so easily? Unlike pedantic instruction, sentence diagramming, and dull drill sheets, these skits made learning the parts of speech entertaining and memorable.

Like Schoolhouse Rock, this book aims to make learning the parts of speech fun. You will find mini-books to make and share, innovative lesson plans, cards, board games, spinners and other manipulatives, and top-notch reproducibles. In addition, the book spells out all the grammar rules related to parts of speech, so you won't have to look elsewhere for pertinent information.

By the end of this hands-on unit, your students should be able to name and give examples of most of the major parts of speech—nouns, verbs, adjectives, adverbs, and pronouns. They will understand that these parts of speech are the building blocks of language—and they'll be able to make the most of these building blocks in their own writing.

You can use the activities and mini-lessons in any order you like. Just check the label at the top of each lesson to see which major concepts are being explored. Other teaching tips follow.

✳ Distribute copies of the grammar Workshop pages (found at the beginning of each chapter) for students to refer to as they complete the activities in this book. Students can bind these pages together and add a cover to make a handy mini grammar reference book.

✳ Have students work on some of the activities in collaborative groups. Students will learn from and build on one another's ideas.

✳ Use the poster included in this book as the centerpiece of an exciting parts-of-speech bulletin board or learning corner. See page 6 for a fun way to get started.

✳ Provide plenty of opportunities for students to share their work with classmates, parents, and others. For example, after you have played a game of Verb Charades at school, encourage students to play a round at home. (Include a note explaining the purpose of the game.) Or invite another class to visit and create parts-of-speech partner stories together. With many of these activities, repetition is the key to learning. Students won't want to put their games and creations aside!

Teaching With the Poster: "The Parts-of-Speech Rap"

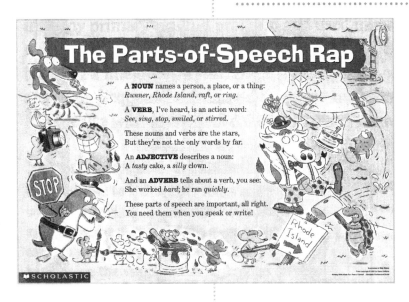

Make grammar the main attraction in your classroom by displaying the poster included in this book. It features an original rhyme called "The Parts-of-Speech Rap." The poem is designed to assist students in remembering the main parts of speech. Its lively beat and rhyme scheme will have your students rapping all day long.

Hang the poster in a spot where students can see it from their seats. Recite the poem several times together, and then explore it with your class. Point out that the words in italics are examples of the part of speech being described. Invite students to name other examples of nouns, verbs, adjectives, and adverbs, and list them in columns on the chalkboard or on chart paper.

To make the most of the poem, give students individual copies (see page 7). If you are using the two companion books in this series (*Capitalization, Punctuation & Spelling* and *Sentences and Paragraphs*), distribute copies of the poems in those books as well. Have students make a grammar poem book by binding the rhymes together and adding a cover.

Chances are, your class is not the only one in your school studying or reviewing the parts of speech. Consider having your students perform "The Parts-of-Speech Rap" for another class or for the whole school. Students can wear costumes and act out the examples named in the poem. For example, one student might dress as a runner and carry the Rhode Island flag. Another might mime the verb *stirred* by stirring a spoon in a bowl. Even if you can't organize an audience, have students record their performance on video or audiotape.

The Parts-of-Speech Rap

A **NOUN** names a person, a place, or a thing:
Runner, Rhode Island, raft, or ring.

A **VERB**, I've heard, is an action word:
See, sing, stop, smiled, or stirred.

These nouns and verbs are the stars,
But they're not the only words by far.

An **ADJECTIVE** describes a noun:
A tasty cake, a silly clown.

And an **ADVERB** tells about a verb, you see:
She worked hard; he ran quickly.

These parts of speech are important, all right.
You need them when you speak or write!

ILLUSTRATION BY MIKE MORAN   Poem copyright © 2001 by Karen Kellaher   *Writing Skills Made Fun: Parts of Speech*   Scholastic Professional Books

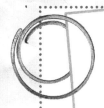

Noun Workshop

A noun is a word that names a person, place, or thing.
Nouns can be common or proper.

 A **common noun** does not name a particular person, place, or thing and does not begin with a capital letter.

student	store	holiday
aunt	state	car
leader	park	game

 A **proper noun** names a particular person, place, or thing, and always begins with a capital letter:

Martin	QuickShop	Thanksgiving
Aunt Betty	Iowa	Honda
George Washington	Elmwood Park	Candyland

 Nouns can be singular or plural. There are several rules for making a singular noun plural:

- Add *-s* to the end of most nouns. For example: *cat/cats, umbrella/umbrellas*.
- Add *-es* to the end of a noun ending in *ch, s, sh, x,* or *z*. For example: *church/churches, loss/losses*.
- Drop the *-y* and add *-ies* to to a noun ending in a consonant followed by *-y*. For example: *penny/pennies, candy/candies*.
- Change *f* to *v* and add *-es* to many nouns ending in *f* or *fe*. For example: *knife/knives, thief/thieves*.
- Some nouns change in unpredictable ways when they become plural. For example, *child/children, foot/feet*.
- Some nouns do not change when they become plural. For example, *deer/deer, sheep/sheep*.

 Some nouns are made up of two or more words put together. These are called compound nouns or compound words. Examples include:

thunderstorm	teardrop	bumblebee
sunshine	dishwasher	daydream
firefighter	baseball	sunset

Noun Activities

The Noun Name Game

Name	People	Places	Things

Once you've reviewed different types of nouns with students, let them practice coming up with examples. A fun way to do this is the Noun Name Game. On the chalkboard, copy the grid format, right. Provide students with pencils and paper and instruct them to copy the chart. Then direct students' attention to the column of blank lines under the heading "Name." Tell students to write each letter in their first name on these lines. If a student has an especially long name, suggest that he or she use a middle or last name or even his or her initials. Once students have filled in their names, invite them to fill in the grid with people, places, and things that begin with the letters in their name. Remind students that they can—and may well need to—use both common and proper nouns. Here's an example of a completed grid:

Name	People	Places	Things
C	child	closet	cat
A	Anna	Alabama	apple
R	Ryan	Rhode Island	rope
A	aunt	attic	alligator

To challenge students, set a timer for two or three minutes and have them stop writing when the timer goes off. Then review the students' answers by going through the alphabet. For example, say, "Who has an *a* in his or her name? What nouns did you come up with?" Make a list of all the nouns students name for each letter. Your list will show students' imaginations at work. Consider saving the list and using it as a reference when you make the Noun Alphabet Quilt (see activity below).

Noun Alphabet Quilt

A student-created noun quilt makes a colorful decoration for your classroom and serves as an instant reminder of what nouns do. This activity is designed for classes with 26 or more students but can be easily adapted for smaller groups.

You Will Need

* a standard-size sheet of posterboard
* 30 construction-paper squares, 4 by 4 inches each
* markers or crayons

them sky We
are I see icy I am -er Ted

What to Do

1 Distribute one square to each student. Assign each student a letter of the alphabet. If you have fewer than 26 students, ask some students to work on two letters. If you have more than 26 students, have students work in pairs.

2 Each student should write his or her letter in the square, followed by a noun that begins with that letter. Students should also illustrate their nouns in the squares. Remind students that they can use all kinds of nouns: common, proper, singular, and plural.

3 Assemble the quilt by pasting the letters in alphabetical order on the posterboard. You should fit five squares across and six squares down, with a bit of room to spare. Because there are 30 squares and only 26 letters, you will have four extra squares. I recommend labeling these squares "Our Noun Quilt" and placing them at the top or in the center of the quilt.

4 Display the quilt for the whole school to admire!

Nouns Go to School

To help students begin to realize just how many different nouns there are in the English language, have them label all the nouns they can find in your classroom or school. Provide sticky notes in three different colors: one for people, one for places, and one for things. Then divide the class into small groups and assign each group a section of your school or classroom. Students should label the nouns they see. Examples include:

DESK	BATHROOM	SAMUEL
COAT	CAFETERIA	TEACHER
CHAIR	COATROOM	PRINCIPAL
FLOOR	CLASSROOM	FOURTH-GRADER
WINDOW	READING CORNER	ROSITA

Have each group tell the class about the nouns they found. Award a prize to the group with the most nouns.

Explore More!

This activity also works well with magazine and book illustrations. Simply have students label the nouns they find in the pictures.

Melvin's Amazing Noun Multiplying Machine (Use with Kids' Page 14.)

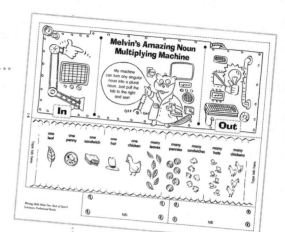

This "slider" manipulative lets children explore the rules for forming plurals in a fun and relaxing way. Best of all, constructing the slider requires just a few snips of the scissors!

You Will Need

* a copy of page 14 for each student
* scissors
* markers or crayons
* tape or glue stick

What to Do

1 Discuss the rules for forming plurals and write some examples on the board.

2 Provide each student with a copy of the reproducible. Direct them to cut out the two panels—the multiplying machine and the noun strip. Also have them cut out the two rectangular tabs and set them aside.

3 Tell students to carefully cut along the two vertical dotted lines on the multiplying machine to make two slits. Students may need your help with this step. (An easy way to cut the slits is to fold the paper at a right angle to the dotted cut lines. Then snip along the lines from the crease of the fold inward.)

4 Model how to slide the noun strip through the left hand slit on the multiplying machine and under the machine. Then slide the noun strip back up through the right hand slit.

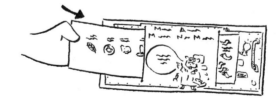

5 To keep the noun strip from sliding out of the machine, students can tape or glue one tab to each end of the noun strip.

6 To use the machine, students pull the left side of the noun strip all the way to the left. They will see all of the singular nouns in a row, about to enter the machine. When they pull the noun strip to the right, they can watch as each singular noun magically becomes plural!

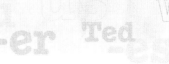

Compound Words Lift-the-Flap Book

(Use with Kids' Page 15–16.)

When students begin to read and write multisyllable words, they are often delighted to discover that two nouns can sometimes be put together to make one compound noun. For example, *tear* plus *drop* becomes *teardrop*; *sun* plus *burn* becomes *sunburn*. Help students understand this concept by making and sharing the "lift the flap" book on pages 15–16.

You Will Need

✳ double-sided copy of pages 15–16 for each student

✳ markers or crayons

✳ scissors

What to Do

1 Provide each student with a copy of the reproducible.

2 Share some examples of compound nouns, and invite students to name the two smaller words that make up each noun: *sunset, baseball, firefighter,* and so on.

3 Have students cut out the pattern along the outer dotted lines and place Side B faceup. Fold the right and left edges of the page in along the solid vertical lines. The two edges should meet in the middle. Crease well.

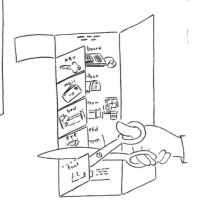

4 Cut along the dotted lines to create doors, or flaps.

5 Together, read the two nouns on the front of the book, then open the flaps to reveal the compound noun inside. Repeat with each compound noun.

6 For the last set of words on the page, *foot* and *ball*, invite students to name the noun that is formed when the two words are put together. Have them lift the flaps and then write and illustrate the word inside.

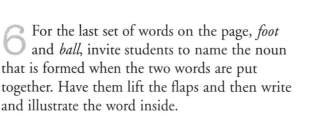

Presto Change-o!: A Proper Noun Pop-Up Book (Use with Kids' Pages 17–18)

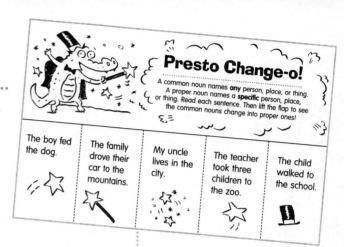

This hands-on activity will help students distinguish between common and proper nouns.

You Will Need

✳ a double-sided copy of pages 17–18 for each student

✳ scissors

✳ glue or tape

✳ markers or crayons

What to Do

1 Provide each student with a copy of the double-sided reproducible. Then guide them in following these instructions:

✳ Cut out the pattern along the outer dotted lines on page 17.

✳ Cut along the four dotted lines on Side A to create five flaps.

✳ Fold the pattern in half along the center horizontal line. Crease the fold well. To keep the page folded, put a drop of glue or a bit of tape toward the top of each side. Do not glue or tape the flaps you have cut.

2 Invite students to color the page. Then tell them to read the sentence on the front of each flap, open the flap, and read the sentence inside. Presto Change-o! Common nouns are transformed into proper nouns, right before their eyes!

3 Challenge students to perform their own magic on the last two sentences by changing the common nouns to proper nouns.

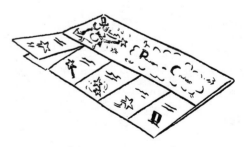

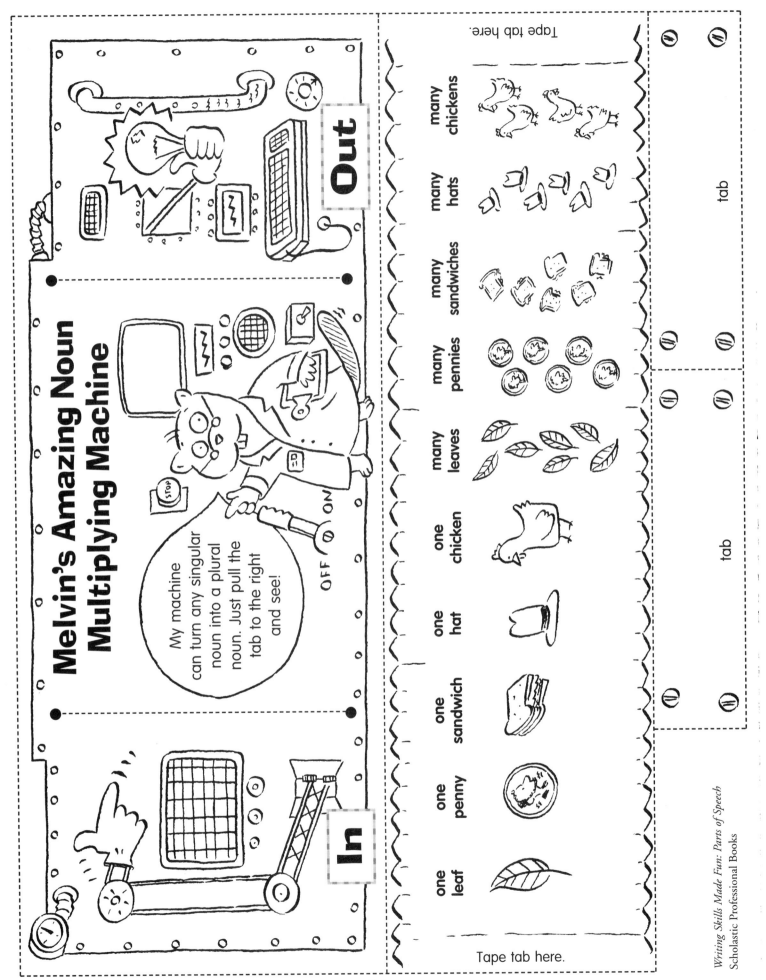

Writing Skills Made Fun: Parts of Speech
Scholastic Professional Books

Nouns

board

box

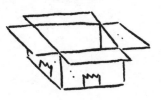

room

lid

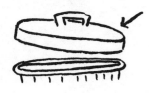

ball

Compound

key

mail

bed

eye

foot

Writing Skills Made Fun: Parts of Speech Scholastic Professional Books

Compound nouns are made up of
two smaller nouns.

keyboard

 mailbox

bedroom

 eyelid

 **It's your turn!** Put the two nouns together to make a compound noun.

Writing Skills Made Fun: Parts of Speech Scholastic Professional Books

Presto Change-o!

A common noun names **any** person, place, or thing.
A proper noun names a **specific** person, place,
or thing. Read each sentence. Then lift the flap to see
the common nouns change into proper ones!

The boy fed the dog.

The family drove their car to the mountains.

My uncle lives in the city.

The teacher took three children to the zoo.

The child walked to the school.

_____   _____

_____   _____

_____   _____

_____   _____

_____   _____

Your turn!   **Your turn!**
Rewrite the sentence   Rewrite the sentence
using proper nouns.   using proper nouns.

My Uncle   The Wilsons   Charlie fed
Peter lives   drove their   Fido.
in New   Jeep to the
York City.   Rocky
                Mountains.

Writing Skills Made Fun: Parts of Speech Scholastic Professional Books

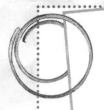

Pronoun Workshop

A pronoun is a word that takes the place of a noun in naming a person, place, or thing.

 There are several types of pronouns, but personal pronouns are the most commonly used.

The personal pronouns are:

I	you	he	it	we	they
me	your	him	its	us	them
my	yours	his		our	their
mine		she		ours	theirs
		her			
		hers			

 Here are some examples of personal pronouns in action:

<u>I</u> went to the store with Pedro.
<u>I</u> went to the store with <u>him</u>.

<u>You</u> and Baxter sing well together.
<u>You</u> and <u>he</u> sing well together.

Tina gave <u>Kai</u> a birthday present.
<u>She</u> gave <u>him</u> a birthday present.

<u>My</u> family gave Tina a gift, too.
<u>We</u> gave <u>her</u> a gift, too.

This is the Cranes' house.
This is <u>their</u> house.

Pronoun Activities

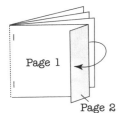

The Pronoun Sisters' Tongue Twister
Mini-Book (Use with Kids' Pages 21–22.)

This activity provides a humorous context in which to explore the role of personal pronouns. Children construct a book of tongue twisters, then use their grammar smarts to replace the nouns in each with appropriate pronouns. After the grammar exercise has been completed, your students will have a fun keepsake—a book of their own to share with family and friends.

You Will Need

* double-sided copy of pages 21–22 for each student
* markers or crayons
* pencils
* scissors

What to Do

1. Tell students to place page 21 faceup on the desk. Then guide them in following these directions:

   * Cut out the patterns along the outer dotted lines.
   * Cut along the dotted horizontal line to make two rectangular panels.
   * Fold each panel in half along the solid center line. Nestle the folded pages inside one another so that the pages go in order from 1 to 8. Staple the left edge of the book to bind it.
   * Find the dotted vertical lines on pages 2, 4, 6, and 8. Fold in along these lines (fold to the left).

2. As students read the book, they can lift the folded edges of the pages to see how each tongue twister would read if its nouns were replaced with pronouns. Point out to students that modifiers for the nouns, such as adjectives and articles, have also been replaced. On Mini-Book page 7, students provide the necessary pronouns.

Pick-a-Pronoun Word
Search (Use with Kids' Page 23.)

Let children tackle a puzzle while learning about pronouns. Have children fill in the missing pronoun in each sentence. Then invite them to find and circle the pronouns in the word-search puzzle.

The Pronoun Sisters' Tongue Twister Mini-Book

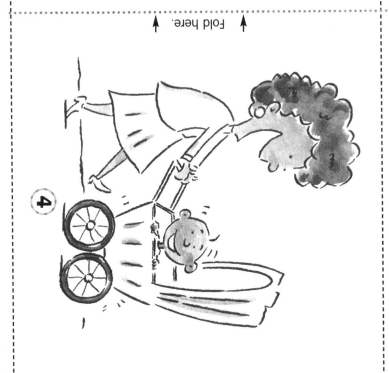

④

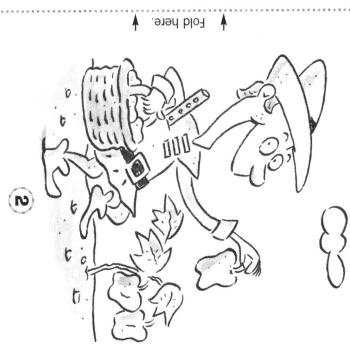

②

Fold here. ↑ ↑ Fold here.

Fold here. ↑ ↑ Fold here.

Read the tongue twisters. Replace the nouns with pronouns from the box.

1. She sells **seashells**.

She sells _____.

2. Fuzzy Wuzzy was a bear.

_____ was a bear.

⑦

Good job!

⑤

Betty brought **the baby buggy** to **the Bunkers**.

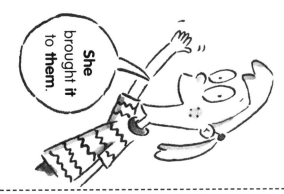

She brought **it** to **them**.

Writing Skills Made Fun: Parts of Speech Scholastic Professional Books

Kids' Page

Pick-a-Pronoun

Word Search

Read each set of sentences. Fill in the blank with a pronoun from the box. Then find your answers in the puzzle. Words can go across or down.

T	H	E	Y	M	A	Z
H	O	P	C	V	U	I
I	W	B	Q	H	E	T
M	S	H	E	L	P	D
K	E	F	H	J	N	O
H	E	R	S	F	E	I

1. <u>Maria</u> likes apples.

_____ likes apples.

2. I met <u>John</u> at school.

I met _____ at school.

3. Put the <u>backpack</u> on the floor.

Put _____ on the floor.

4. <u>The students</u> can't wait for lunch.

_____ can't wait for lunch.

5. That bike is <u>Kate's</u>.

That bike is _____ .

Pronoun Box

I
you
he
she
it
we
you
they
me
him
hers
us
them

Writing Skills Made Fun: Parts of Speech Scholastic Professional Books

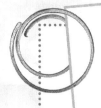

Verb Workshop

A verb is a word that shows action or a state of being.

 An **action verb** is a verb that shows physical or mental action. You can usually find the action verb in a sentence by asking "What did the person, place, or thing *do*?"

smile	taste	grow
run	read	like
call	paint	fly

 A **linking verb** is a verb that shows a state of being. It does not show action. Linking verbs link the subject to other words in a sentence. Here are some examples:

Leonard <u>is</u> my best friend.   I <u>am</u> happy.
Pandas <u>are</u> endangered.   The sky <u>seems</u> dark.

The tense of a verb tells the reader or listener when the action or state of being takes place.

 The **present tense** expresses an action that takes place in the present. For example:

The store <u>is</u> open.   I <u>write</u> poems.   The sun <u>shines</u> on us.

 The **past tense** expresses an action that has already taken place. Most verbs are regular: To form the past tense -*d* or -*ed* is added. For example:

Hannah <u>skipped</u> down the block.   We <u>danced</u> together.

 Other verbs are irregular: To form the past tense, their spelling changes in unpredictable ways.

Lily <u>wore</u> a blue hat.
Patrick <u>was</u> late for school.
We <u>won</u> the game last Saturday.

The **future tense** expresses an action that will take place in the future. It has not happened yet. For example:

Chris <u>will watch</u> the movie.
We <u>will walk</u> home together.
It <u>will rain</u> tomorrow.

Verb Activities

Verb Charades

To help convey to students that many verbs express an action, play a rousing game of verb charades. Write each of the words listed below on a small slip of paper. Fold the slips of paper and put them in a bowl or hat. Invite one student at a time to take a verb from the hat and act it out for the rest of the class. Just as in traditional charades, the student cannot give spoken hints. The trick to this version of the game, however, is that students must give the answer in verb form. For example, if the verb is *paint*, then the words *painter* and *paintbrush* are not acceptable answers.

Have students write their own verbs to put in the hat!

climb	read	give	throw
whisper	erase	laugh	clean
dig	swim	paint	write
think	carry	pack	play
grow	call	share	ride
count	cook	wake	turn

Sound-Verbs Story Starters (Use with Kids' Page 27.)

An effectively-written story engages all of the reader's senses. Carefully chosen words help the reader experience the story as if he or she were really there. An enjoyable way to convey this writing rule to second- and third-grade writers is to explore what I call "sound verbs." The meaning of these verbs is conveyed through the way they sound. For example, the verb *cackle* sounds a lot like a cackle. The verb *hoot* sounds like something hooting.

Have students use page 27 to practice using these verbs. Students should pick one of three story starters and write a short story using some of the sound verbs in the box. You'll be amazed at the different stories kids come up with—and students will begin to understand the power of a well-chosen verb!

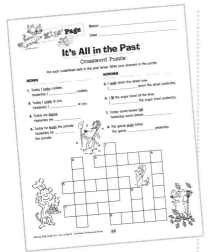

It's All in the Past Crossword Puzzle

(Use with Kids' Page 28.)

When students tackle this crossword, they'll get great practice putting verbs in the past tense. Before distributing the puzzle, review the rules for forming the past tense. This activity focuses on verbs that form the past tense by adding -ed, but it also includes several irregular verbs (*sit/sat, leads/led*). For students who have never completed a crossword before, provide some helpful hints:

✳ You can skip a clue and go back to it later. Sometimes when you write down one answer, one of its letters appears in another answer. That gives you a head start!

✳ If you are not sure if you have the right answer, try counting the number of spaces provided for that answer in the puzzle. If that number matches the number of letters in your answer, you may have the right answer.

Kate's Vacation

(Use with Kids' Page 29.)

Explore the future tense with this fun exercise. Explain that Kate wrote her diary entry before she went on a big vacation. It's your students' job to make sure all of Kate's verbs are in the future tense. Students should underline the future-tense verb in each parenthetical set.

My Day at the Zoo: A Fill-in-the-Blanks Partner Story (Use with Kids' Page 30.)

Kids love nonsense stories—and if it's a silly story they created themselves, all the better! For this activity, divide the class into pairs and designate one student in each pair as the writer. The other student is the word-giver. Distribute a copy of the reproducible to each writer—but don't let the word-giver catch a glimpse or the surprise will be spoiled. To begin, the writer will ask the word-giver to name seven verbs. Some will be in the present tense, some in the past tense, and some in the future tense. If the word-giver follows directions and has studied his or her verb tenses, the result will be a side-splitting tale.

Invite each pair to share its funny story with the class. To give all students practice in naming verbs, have students switch roles for another round.

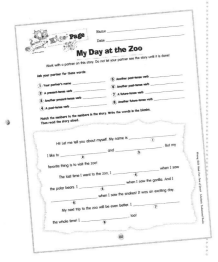

Name _____

Date _____

Using Sound Verbs

You can guess the meaning of some verbs just by listening to how they sound. For example, the verb <u>groan</u> sounds just like a groan! Pick one of the story starters below. Write a story using some of the verbs from the box.

Verbs

hoot	crash	roar	cackle	shriek	whistle
groan	moo	gulp	sigh	hiss	sniff
rattle	chirp	plop	ring	squeak	sizzle

Story Starters

1 You are camping in the woods with your family. You take a walk to find wood for the campfire.

2 It's your birthday. You are looking forward to a special day, but everything starts to go wrong!

3 A hot-air balloon lands in your school yard. A famous person steps out and says hello.

Kids' Page

Name _____

Date _____

It's All in the Past

Crossword Puzzle

Put each underlined verb in the past tense. Write your answers in the puzzle.

DOWN

1. Today I <u>bake</u> cookies.
Yesterday I _____ cookies.

2. Today I <u>smile</u> at you.
Yesterday I _____ at you.

4. Today we <u>dance</u>.
Yesterday we _____ .

6. Today he <u>leads</u> the parade.
Yesterday he _____
the parade.

ACROSS

3. I <u>walk</u> down the street now.
I _____ down the street yesterday.

5. I <u>fill</u> the sugar bowl all the time.
I _____ the sugar bowl yesterday.

7. Today some leaves <u>fall</u>.
Yesterday some leaves _____ .

8. The game <u>ends</u> today.
The game _____ yesterday.

Name _____

Date _____

Kate's Vacation

Kate is going on a trip next week. She wrote about her plans in her diary. Since Kate's trip will happen in the future, make sure her verbs are in the future tense. Underline the correct verb in each sentence.

Dear Diary,

   I (**left, will leave**) for the beach next Monday. I am so excited! I (**will play, played**) in the ocean. I (**eat, will eat**) ice cream on the beach. I (**will build, built**) sand castles, too!

   At night I (**will watch, watched**) the sun set. Then I (**rode, will ride**) the giant roller coaster. I (**will take, took**) pictures of everything to show my friends back home. I (**buy, will buy**) a treat to share with them, too!

Name _____

Date _____

My Day at the Zoo

Work with a partner on this story. Do not let your partner see the story until it is done!

Ask your partner for these words:

1 Your partner's name _____

2 A present-tense verb _____

3 Another present-tense verb _____

4 A past-tense verb _____

5 Another past-tense verb _____

6 Another past-tense verb _____

7 A future-tense verb _____

8 Another future-tense verb _____

Match the numbers to the numbers in the story. Write the words in the blanks. Then read the story aloud.

Hi! Let me tell you about myself. My name is _____ .
1

I like to _____ and _____ . But my
2   **3**

favorite thing is to visit the zoo!

The last time I went to the zoo, I _____ when I saw
4

the polar bears. I _____ when I saw the gorilla. And I
5

_____ when I saw the snakes! It was an exciting day.
6

My next trip to the zoo will be even better. I _____
7

the whole time! I _____ , too!
8

Writing Skills Made Fun: Parts of Speech   Scholastic Professional Books

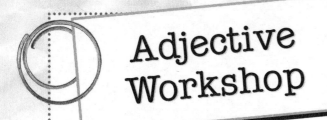

Adjective Workshop

An adjective is a word that describes a noun or pronoun.

❋ Some adjectives answer the question *How many*?

ten apples   many people   four sisters

❋ Some adjectives answer the question *Which one (or ones)*?

this pencil   those sneakers

❋ Some adjectives answer the question *What kind*?

a blue sweater   heavy boxes   Swiss cheese
a kind neighbor   an awful day   the tired children

Adjectives can be used to compare things. Here's how:

❋ Some adjectives describe only one thing:

It is a hot day
Hannah's story is interesting.

❋ Some adjectives are used when two things are being compared.
These adjectives end in *-er* or use the word *more*.

Today is hotter than yesterday.
Hannah's story is more interesting than the first one I read.

❋ Some adjectives are used when three or more things are being
compared. They end in *-est* or use the word *most*.

Today is the hottest day of the summer.
Hannah's story is the most interesting of all.

Adjective Activities

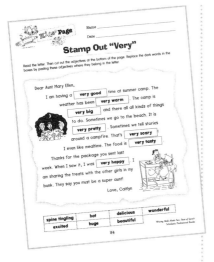

Stamp Out "Very" (Use with Kids' Page 34.)

Tired of reading students' stories filled with the word *very*? Use this reproducible to help kids come up with more colorful and specific adjectives. Point out to students that although the word *very* is perfectly acceptable, overusing it can make our writing boring. Give some examples:

✳ What sounds better: a *very big* ice cream cone OR a *humongous* ice cream cone?

✳ Which sounds worse: a *very bad* day OR a *terrible* day?

✳ Which would you rather be: *very smart* OR *brilliant*?

Then invite students to try the activity on page 34. Students read the letter, then paste an adjective from the box above each boldface phrase. Remind students to read the entire letter and all adjectives before starting to paste.

short
wide
skinny
wet
colorful
icy
hot
striped
happy
upside down
flying
dark
light
round

Adjective Art Mobile

The descriptive nature of adjectives will be more apparent to students when they draw words and decorate them to look like their meanings. On the chalkboard, copy the adjectives *tall* and *fast*, as shown below. Then ask students to describe what they notice about the way the words are written. (*The word* tall *is written long and narrow to look as if the word itself were tall. The motion lines on the word* fast *and its slant make it look like it's going somewhere in a hurry.*) Invite students to think of other adjectives they could illustrate in this fashion. (Some suggestions are given in the word box, left). Then go for it!

Once students have created a rough draft, pass out colored paper and have them produce final versions to display in the classroom. You can make mobiles out of the adjectives by punching holes in them and using yarn to attach them to clothes hangers.

All-About-Me Adjective Banner (Use with Kids' Page 35.)

What better way to explore adjectives than to use them to describe oneself? Have each student think of four adjectives that describe him or her. Then distribute the reproducible and tell students to write their names in the center of the figure. Next, have them write their adjectives on the arms and legs. If they'd like, students can add facial features and yarn hair to their figures. Finally, let them cut out their figures and hang them in a row along the top of your chalkboard or around the edge of your bulletin board.

Lights, Camera, Adjectives!

(Use with Kids' Page 36.)

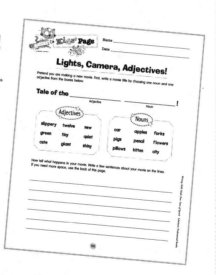

In this activity your students will have a ball using adjectives and nouns to create make-believe movie titles. The activity is an ideal way to show how adjectives and nouns work together to paint a vivid, specific image. It's also a great creative writing exercise that students will beg to do again and again!

Have students follow the directions on the reproducible to come up with an original movie title. Then instruct them to write a short summary of the movie's plot in the space provided. If students need a little guidance in writing the summary, invite them to consider the following questions:

✳ What kind of movie is it (funny, scary, and so on)?

✳ What happens in the movie?

✳ Where does your movie take place?

✳ Who are the main characters in the movie?

✳ How does the movie end?

Encourage students to create movie posters for their films. Each poster should include the title of the movie and an illustration of an interesting or important scene. Some children may want to add a brief "teaser" to get people excited about the film. An example of a teaser is "You won't believe your eyes" or "The funniest movie in years."

Name _____

Date _____

Stamp Out "Very"

Read the letter. Then cut out the adjectives at the bottom of the page. Replace the dark words in the boxes by pasting these adjectives where they belong in the letter.

Dear Aunt Mary Ellen,

I am having a **very good** time at summer camp. The weather has been **very warm**. The camp is **very big** and there all all kinds of things to do. Sometimes we go to the beach. It is **very pretty**. Sometimes we tell stories around a campfire. That's **very scary**! I even like mealtime. The food is **very tasty**.

Thanks for the package you sent last week. When I saw it, I was **very happy**. I am sharing the treats with the other girls in my bunk. They say you must be a super aunt!

Love, Caitlyn

| spine tingling | hot | delicious | wonderful |
| excited | huge | beautiful | |

Name _____

Date _____

All About Me

Write your name in the center of the body. Then think of four adjectives that describe you. Write them on the arms and legs. Color the figure to look like you.

35

Name _____

Date _____

Lights, Camera, Adjectives!

Pretend you are making a new movie. First, write a movie title by choosing one noun and one adjective from the boxes below.

Tale of the _____ _____ !
Adjective   Noun

Adjectives

slippery	twelve	new
green	tiny	quiet
cute	giant	shiny

Nouns

car	apples	forks
pigs	pencil	flowers
pillows	kitten	city

Now tell what happens in your movie. Write a few sentences about your movie on the lines. If you need more space, use the back of this page.

_____

_____

_____

_____

_____

Writing Skills Made Fun: Parts of Speech   Scholastic Professional Books

Adverb Workshop

An adverb is a word
that tells more about a verb.

❋ Some adverbs answer the question *How*?

The boy cried <u>loudly</u>.   The dog ran <u>quickly</u>.   He worked <u>hard</u> on the sign.

❋ Some adverbs answer the question *When*?

I'll finish my snack <u>later</u>.   The students lined up <u>immediately</u>.

❋ Some adverbs answer the question *Where*?

Please sit <u>here</u>.   We looked <u>everywhere</u>.

Many adverbs end in *-ly*. But remember that not all adverbs do. See the sentences above for some examples. The adverbs *very*, *so*, and *too* are also examples of commonly used adverbs that do not end in *-ly*. These adverbs are used to describe other adverbs, for example, *very hard*.

Adverbs can be used to compare verbs. Here's how:

❋ Some adverbs describe only one action.

Sheila ran <u>fast</u>.   The ride went <u>smoothly</u>.

❋ Some adverbs compare two actions. These adverbs end in *-er* or use the word *more*.

Sheila ran <u>faster</u> than Fred.   This ride went <u>more smoothly</u> than the last one.

❋ Some adverbs are used when comparing three or more actions. These adverbs end in *-est* or use the word *most*.

Of all six runners, Sheila ran <u>fastest</u>.
This ride went <u>most smoothly</u> of the three we tried.

Adverb Activities

Identifying Adverbs

Many young students have a hard time identifying adverbs. Even those who have sailed through your lessons on nouns, verbs, and adjectives may stumble when you reach this part of your unit. (One 8-year-old I know told me she was learning about adjectives and proverbs at school!) One of the easiest ways to help students remember the functions of adverbs is to explain that adverbs answer the questions *How? Where?* and *When?* Then write the following sentences on the chalkboard, and have students practice finding the adverbs.

✳ The baby crawled slowly.

　　(Ask: *How* did the baby crawl?)

✳ Madeline stood straight.

　　(Ask: *How* did Madeline stand?)

✳ I waited there for an hour.

　　(Ask: *Where* did I wait?)

✳ I'll see you later.

　　(Ask: *When* will I see you?)

✳ Please sit here now!

　　(Ask: *Where* should you sit? *When* should you sit?)

Afterward, invite students to find some adverbs in a classroom periodical, textbook, or other printed material. Remind students that they are looking for *single* words that tell how, where, and when. Otherwise, students may find prepositional phrases functioning as adverbs (for example, *The mayor went to city hall*). Though an important part of grammar, such phrases are better saved for the upper-elementary grades.

　If your students are just beginning to learn about grammar and you are concerned that they might become overwhelmed, focus on the question *How?* and have students look only for adverbs that answer that question. That way, they are less likely to come up with prepositional phrases functioning as adverbs.

Spin-an-Adverb Wheel (Use with Kids' Pages 41 and 42.)

Many adjectives can be made into adverbs by adding the letters *-ly*. Explore this concept with kids by making these paper wheels. The manipulative is easy to construct and will help students remember how to form and identify various adverbs.

You Will Need

* copies of each reproducible
* brass fasteners
* markers or crayons
* scissors

What to Do

1 Distribute the reproducibles. Invite students to color the TOP WHEEL and cut out the two wheels.

2 Help each student cut out the two small windows on the TOP WHEEL. To cut, poke the tip of the scissors through the paper, or fold the paper at the window.

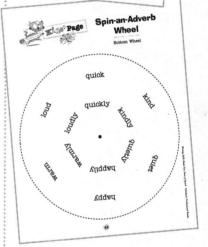

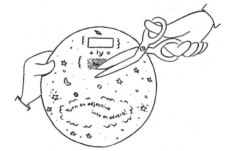

3 Put the TOP WHEEL on top of the BOTTOM WHEEL and and poke a brass fastener through the center of the wheels to fasten them together.

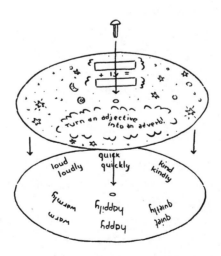

4 Rotate the wheel until an adjective appears in the top window. Consult the bottom window to see the adverb that is formed from that adjective.

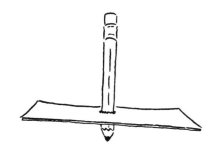

Adverb Action Game (Use with Kids' Page 43.)

One of my older daughter's favorite activities is a board game that requires players to spin their arms, do sit-ups and push-ups, and perform other physical activities. Chances are, you have a few kids in your class who, like my daughter, learn best by doing and moving. Here's a grammar game that taps into their endless energy and enthusiasm. With each turn, students practice putting verbs and adverbs together and then physically demonstrate the meaning of each verb-adverb pair. Here's how to play:

You Will Need

* copies of page 43
* cardboard or posterboard
* glue sticks
* pencils

Get Ready to Play

1 Divide the class into groups of three or four. Distribute the top half of page 43 to each group.

2 Have each group glue the two squares on the reproducible (the verb spinner and the adverb spinner) to posterboard. Then, they cut out the spinner squares.

3 Students then poke a pencil through the center of each square to make a spinner.

How to Play

1 Think of a fair way to decide who will go first (the person whose birthday is coming up next, for example).

2 Distribute a copy of the bottom half of page 43 (the scorecard) to each student.

3 The first player spins both spinners. (The student should twirl the pencil between his or her fingers as if spinning a top.) He or she notes which word on each spinner lands "faceup" (the word opposite the one that touches the desk). The player then does what the two spinners direct him or her to do. For example, if the spinner displays the verb *stand* and the adverb *slowly*, he must stand up slowly. If the spinner displays the verb *clap* and the adverb *happily*, he or she must clap hands with a smile on his or her face.

4 With each turn, players record on the scorecard the verb and adverb they spin. The first player to spin all the verbs and all the adverbs wins.

Cut out

+ ly =

Cut out

Turn an adjective into an adverb!

Spin-an-Adverb Wheel

Bottom Wheel

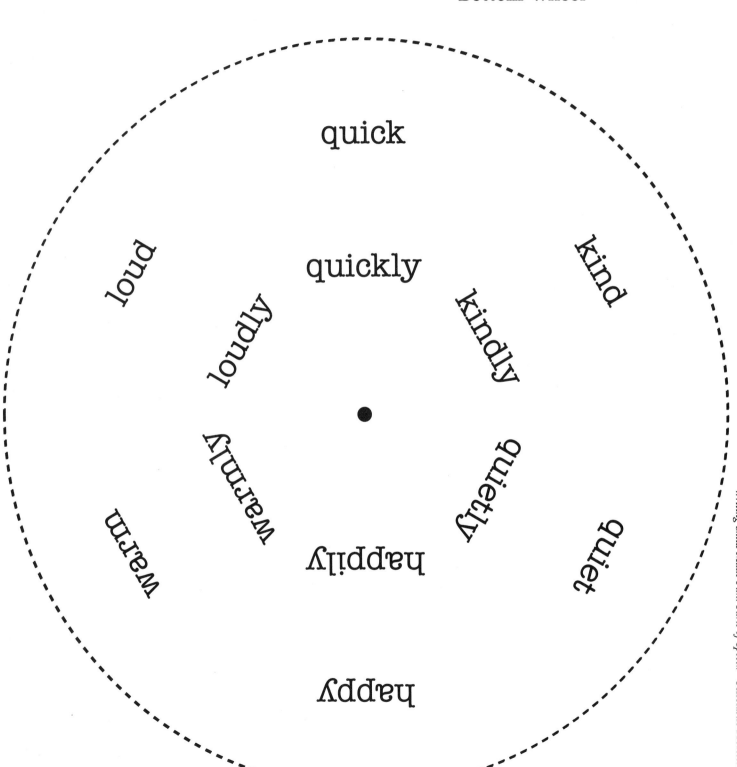

quick

kind

loud

quickly

kindly

loudly

quietly

warmly

happily

warm

happy

quiet

Writing Skills Made Fun: Parts of Speech Scholastic Professional Books

Name _____

Date _____

Adverb Action Spinners

Glue these squares onto cardboard. Then cut them out. Poke a pencil through the middle of each square. Use these spinners to play the Adverb Action game!

Writing Skills Made Fun: Parts of Speech Scholastic Professional Books

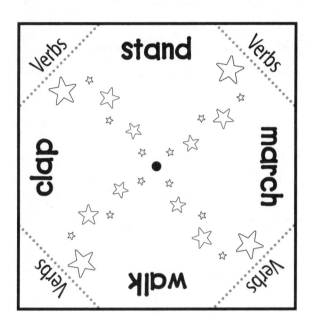

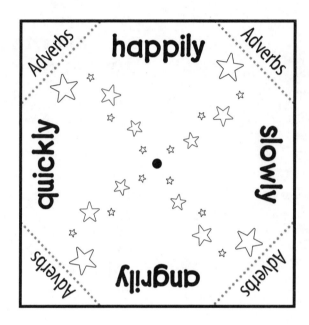

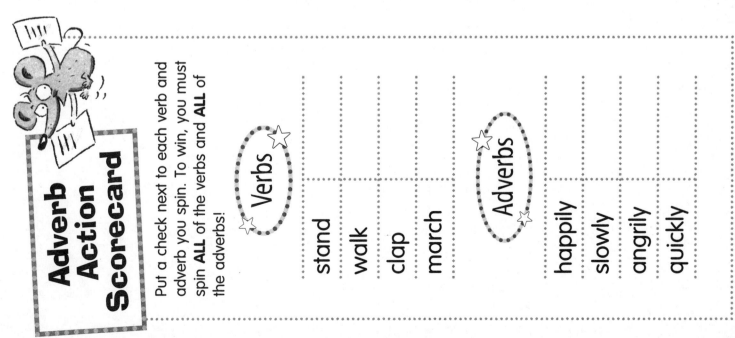

Adverb Action Scorecard

Put a check next to each verb and adverb you spin. To win, you must spin **ALL** of the verbs and **ALL** of the adverbs!

Verbs
- stand
- walk
- clap
- march

Adverbs
- happily
- slowly
- angrily
- quickly

Wrap up your unit on the parts of speech by engaging students in activities that use the parts of speech in combination. The activities in this section demonstrate that the parts of speech do not function in isolation; we must put them all together to express ideas.

My Favorite Food: A Fill-in-the-Blanks Partner Story (Use with Kids' Page 46.)

Students have had some practice with this type of activity (see page 26 of the Verbs section). Now it's time to throw all the parts of speech together and see what happens!

To begin, divide the class into pairs and designate one student in each group to be the writer. The other student is the word-giver. Distribute a copy of the reproducible to each writer—but don't let the word-giver catch a glimpse or the surprise will be spoiled! To begin, the writer will ask the word-giver to name ten words. Some will be nouns, some will be verbs, some will be adjectives, and some will be adverbs.

When students have completed their stories, invite each pair to share its funny story with the class. To give all students practice in naming the parts of speech, have students switch roles for another round!

Parts of Speech in the News

Ask students to bring in articles from newspapers or magazines. Provide highlighters or crayons in five different colors, then create a color key for the parts of speech you have studied. For example:

* Yellow: Nouns
* Pink: Pronouns
* Orange: Verbs
* Blue: Adjectives
* Green: Adverbs

Have students use the color key to underline or highlight the parts of speech they find in their article.

Parts-of-Speech Match-Ups (Use with Kids' Page 47.)

Use this kid-friendly card game to review the five parts of speech you have studied and encourage students to boost their powers of concentration. Play the game with groups of two to four students.

You Will Need

✳ one copy of page 47 for each group

✳ scissors

What to Do

1 Have students cut out the cards and shuffle them.

2 Students then place the cards facedown on the desk, floor, or table, and arrange them in rows.

3 Have students take turns drawing two cards. Students should read the two words aloud and name the part of speech each represents. If the two words are the same part of speech, the student gets to keep the cards and take another turn. If the parts of speech do not match, the student must put the cards facedown in the same spots. It's important that all players get a look at the cards before they are returned to the table.

4 Stroll around the room as students play, and offer assistance as needed. The game ends when all cards have been drawn. The student with the most matches is the winner.

Name _____

Date _____

My Favorite Food

Work with a partner on this story. Do not let your partner see the story until it is done!

Ask your partner to name one word for each of the following parts of speech:

1. Adjective _____
2. Noun (singular or plural) _____
3. Adjective _____
4. Plural noun _____
5. Adjective _____

6. Singular noun _____
7. Present-tense verb _____
8. Adjective _____
9. Present-tense verb _____
10. Adverb _____

Match the numbers to the numbers in the story. Write the words in the blanks.
Then read the story aloud.

What's your favorite food? Mine is _____
①

_____ covered in _____ gravy.
②   ③

It's delicious, and it's not hard to make. To make the gravy, all you need are a few

_____ and a _____ _____.
④   ⑤   ⑥

Start by putting those in a pan. Then _____ the pan until the
⑦

ingredients are _____. Let it cool for a minute, then grab a
⑧

spoon and _____ the mixture as _____
⑨   ⑩

as you can. Enjoy!

Writing Skills Made Fun: Parts of Speech Scholastic Professional Books

desk	pig	won	cute	see
smiled	heavy	it	they	she
girl	blue	proudly	sadly	his
ran	softly	playfully	book	old

Additional Resources

Books

The Amazing Pop-Up Grammar Book by Jennie Maizels, illustrator, and Kate Petty, contributor (Dutton, 1996).

Elementary, My Dear: Caught 'Ya, Grammar With a Giggle for Grades One, Two, and Three by Jane Bell Kiester (Maupin House, 2000).

Grammar Puzzles and Games Kids Can't Resist by Karen Kellaher (Scholastic Professional Books, 2000).

Great Grammar Mini-Books by Maria Fleming (Scholastic Professional Books, 1999).

Hairy, Scary, Ordinary: What Is an Adjective?; A Mink, a Fink, a Skating Rink: What Is a Noun?; and To Root, To Toot, to Parachute: What Is a Verb? all by Brian P. Cleary (Carolrhoda, 1991–2001).

Kites Sail High: A Book About Verbs; Merry Go Round: A Book About Nouns; Mine, All Mine: A Book About Pronouns; Up, Up and Away: A Book About Adverbs; Many Luscious Lollipops: A Book About Adjectives all by Ruth Heller (Paper Star, 1998).

25 Great Grammar Poems With Activities by Bobbi Katz (Scholastic Professional Books, 1999).

Web Sites

✳ Go to **www.scholastic.com** for online writing activities, tips from authors, and more. The site features sections for teachers and students.

✳ Log on to **www.funbrain.com/grammar/** for exciting grammar games.

✳ For more suggestions on teaching grammar and other language arts topics, check out the site of the National Council of Teachers of English: **www.ncte.org/teach/**.

Video

Grammar Rock (Disney Presents Schoolhouse Rock, 1997). VHS. This video collection features the original rhymes from the late 1970s, including *Unpack Your Adjectives* and *Verbs: That's What's Happening.*

Answers

✳ Pronouns

PICK-A-PRONOUN WORD SEARCH:
1. She; 2. him; 3. it; 4. They; 5. hers.

✳ Verbs

IT'S ALL IN THE PAST CROSSWORD PUZZLE:
DOWN—1. baked; 2. smiled; 4. danced; 6. led.
ACROSS—3. walked; 5. filled; 7. fell; 8. ended.

KATE'S VACATION: will leave, will play, will eat, will build, will watch, will ride, will take, will buy.

✳ Adjectives

STAMP OUT "VERY": very good = wonderful ;
very warm = hot; very big = huge; very pretty = beautiful;
very scary = spine tingling; very tasty = delicious;
very happy = excited.

✳ Review

PARTS-OF-SPEECH MATCH-UPS: VERBS—ran, smiled, see, won. NOUNS—girl, desk, pig, book. ADJECTIVES—blue, heavy, cute, old. ADVERBS—softly, playfully, proudly, sadly. PRONOUNS—it, she, they, his.